MRS EWING

MRS EWING

Mrs Ewing

A WALCK MONOGRAPH

by

Gillian Avery

HENRY Z. WALCK, INCORPORATED
NEW YORK

Library of Congress Catalog Card Number: 64-20838
© The Bodley Head Ltd 1961
First American Edition 1964
Printed in Great Britain

CONTENTS

A Note About the Author

Gillian Avery was born in 1926 at Redhill in Surrey. After leaving school she spent eight years in publishing, beginning with two years on the *Surrey Mirror* as a junior reporter. In 1949 she went to Oxford to the Clarendon Press, as assistant illustrations editor on the Oxford Junior Encyclopaedia, and in 1952 married A. O. J. Cockshut, then Andrew Bradley Fellow at Balliol College, to whom her interest in Victorian literature is largely due.

Her first book, *The Warden's Niece*, a novel for children about Victorian Oxford, was published in 1957, and since then Gillian Avery has written three other novels, *Trespassers at Charlcote*, *James Without Thomas*, and *The Elephant War*—all with a Victorian setting. She has also compiled two anthologies, *The Sapphire Treasury*, which included a number of Victorian works, and *In the Window Seat*, which is a collection of Victorian short stories by such authors as Mrs. Gatty, Ouida, Annie Keary, Charlotte Yonge, and Mrs. Ewing. Her great interest is in Victorian children's novels, and in persuading publishers to reissue some of those whose excellence has been forgotten.

Since 1954 Gillian Avery has lived in Manchester with her husband and small daughter.

1. Mother and Daughter:
Margaret Gatty and Julie Gatty

The history of Juliana Horatia Ewing must begin with the history of her mother, for out of her mother's writing developed the daughter's. She took over her mother's style and technique and though she ended by soaring far beyond her, the beginning had been made by Margaret Gatty.

Margaret Gatty was born in 1809, the daughter of Alexander Scott, chaplain to Nelson, in whose arms Nelson died. The tradition of this connection was proudly preserved by the family; to Ecclesfield Vicarage, where Mrs. Gatty spent the whole of her married life, were brought two black leather armchairs which had come from the *Victory*, and no less than three of her children were christened after Nelson: two girls (including Mrs. Ewing herself), and a boy, Horatio Nelson Gatty, who died in infancy.

Mrs. Gatty's mother died when her two daughters were very small, and for many years the little Margaret and her sister Horatia were shuttled to and fro between their father, who had a living in Essex, and their grandparents' house in the precincts of the Charterhouse in London. Until 1817 they had no permanent home, but in that year Dr. Scott was presented to the living of Catterick in Yorkshire, and the children moved there with him. Throughout her life Margaret Gatty was possessed of immense energy, and as a

9

young girl she studied with the zeal and enthusiasm that one connects with so many of the women writers of that century—from George Eliot to Charlotte Yonge—becoming proficient enough in Italian to do a translation of Dante, teaching herself German, writing verses, sketching, and even attempting to learn Chinese.

She did not marry until 1839. She was finding her life rather melancholy by that time: the friends of her youth with whom she had shared such esoteric interests as demonology and astrology were now scattered, the literary clubs which she and her sister had founded, in abeyance, and family responsibilities heavy upon her. Alfred Gatty, then a curate with many social graces but slender means, came to visit Catterick Vicarage at the invitation of Dr. Scott, who greatly approved of him until he found that the young man had fallen in love with Margaret. On grounds of prudence he opposed the match as implacably as his own father-in-law had originally opposed him. Margaret was more dutiful than her mother (who had escaped over the garden wall to marry Alexander Scott), and told her father that while her own and Alfred Gatty's minds were made up, she would not marry until Dr. Scott gave his consent. Dr. Scott yielded, the couple were married, and before the year was ended good fortune blessed them; a living in the gift of one of Margaret Scott's uncles fell vacant, and the Gattys came north from Alfred Gatty's curacy in Southminster to Ecclesfield

Vicarage, near Sheffield, where Margaret was to spend the rest of her life.

The living was an improvement on the curacy of £57 a year, but even so Mrs. Gatty seems to have found it a struggle. In addition to financial worries of her own she was saddled with the settling up of her father's affairs, and litigation over her grandfather's. And the family increased rapidly; in eleven years Mrs. Gatty had borne nine children, of whom eight survived. To try to bring in a little money Mr. and Mrs. Gatty set about writing a life of Dr. Scott. This was published in 1842 and was well received, but it was not until the 1850's that Mrs. Gatty, child-bearing now over (except for the solitary son that was born and died in 1855), settled down to write in earnest.

In the past, before her marriage, she had written gaily for the literary clubs that she had formed among her friends; now she was grimly applying herself to earning money for the family. Mrs. Ewing wrote of 'the dear Mum's years and years of work and earnings, poured as a matter of course into the leaky bucket of a large family's expenses'. In this lies the great difference between Mrs. Gatty and her daughter; the one wrote, in the midst of heavy family and parish duties, to provide more money for the family and the expensive education of her sons, finding the effort of it great labour; the other, blessed with far more leisure and fewer responsibilities, wrote because she loved it.

11

Surprisingly enough, by the 1850's Mrs. Gatty's deepest interest was not writing, but seaweeds. It was a curious one for an exceedingly busy and harassed woman, living in an inland town with very little money or leisure for travelling, and without any scientific training. It began with a visit to Hastings in 1848, and she managed to master the subject with such effect that by 1863 she was able to publish a two volume work, *The History of British Seaweeds*, which long remained a standard textbook on the subject. Her enthusiasm for her seaweeds was so great that when her first book, *The Fairy Godmothers*, was published in 1851 she asked the publishers, instead of paying her, to give her in exchange a book on zoophytes, and the second edition was paid for by a *History of British Sponges and Lithophytes*, together with five pounds' worth of books.

The beginning of literary success came with the first series of *Parables from Nature*, which long continued to be reprinted, and with which her name nowadays is chiefly connected. The parables were published at intervals over the years, the fifth series not appearing until 1871. They were intended primarily for a child reader, but even Charlotte Yonge considered them difficult for children, and in fact they won their reputation among a far more adult circle.

More popular among children were the Aunt Judy stories—*Aunt Judy's Tales* (1859) and *Aunt Judy's Letters* (1862). Aunt Judy was the family nickname for Juliana Horatia—also known as Julie—who by that time was in her late teens and was the family story-teller. The children in these stories are the Gatty children—referred to by numbers—and their doings are the authentic doings of the Vicarage nursery. So much so that as the children grew into schoolchildren and left the nursery for ever, Mrs. Gatty found that her source of ideas for domestic stories had dried up, and she lacked the invention to think up imaginary children.

At the time when these books appeared Mrs. Gatty was at the peak of her powers; she was contributing regularly to Charlotte Yonge's magazine the *Monthly Packet*, and her books were appearing at the rate of two a year. She was achieving fame and a position in the literary world. The way in which Mrs. Gatty and later Mrs. Ewing were lionized in London is an interesting example of how much more compact Victorian society was and how all-embracing the tastes of the reading public: Queen Victoria and Gladstone read Mrs. Gatty's stories, Lord Tennyson admired them, and through them made her acquaintance, an acquaintance which later deepened into a close friendship.

But in spite of all this fame, financially Mrs. Gatty did not seem to be benefitting very much. Half a crown a page was all she received from the *Monthly Packet*, and every penny she earned was sunk in the family, chiefly, no doubt, in her sons, who were being educated at Eton, Winchester, Marlborough and Charterhouse. Certainly she spent nothing on her own clothes, nor on decorating the house, for in 1862, in the middle of her earning career, she was ruefully talking about the dining room, which had never had curtains, and the drawing room, where the curtains were twenty-one years old. So desperate were financial needs that in 1863 she undertook a laborious translation from French because a payment of twenty guineas was offered, although by that time her health was deteriorating, and her right hand was so painful that she had to write with her left. This was the onset of the creeping paralysis that eventually killed her.

So when in 1866 she was asked by her publishers, Messrs George Bell, to edit a new children's magazine she eagerly accepted. It meant a regular salary of ten pounds a month, and also an opening for the publication of Julie's stories. It would be hard work, but there were four unmarried daughters at home to help with it. The publishers themselves chose the name, after the popular *Aunt Judy's Tales*, which were named after Julie. It seems that later Bell regretted the choice of title, but by that time it was too firmly established to be changed.

Compared to some of its contemporaries, the *Children's Prize*, for instance, or *Chatterbox*, *Aunt Judy* was not over-burdened with improving articles and didactic stories. No magazine that had Julie as a regular contributor could ever be that. And compared to the *Monthly Packet* it was bright indeed. The *Monthly Packet* was heavily loaded with such articles as 'Present Day Thoughts on the Education Problem', and discussions on how a young girl could best allot her time so as to find opportunities for private study. Admittedly the editor of *Aunt Judy* had said in her foreword to the first number:

'Parents need not fear an overflowing of mere amusement. They will find . . . things to be remembered in each month—and these will comprise facts and anecdotes, historical, biographical, or otherwise, deserving a niche in the brain-temple of the young.'

But the articles were mostly about such cheerfully factual matters as the habits of snakes, or a Red Indian tribe, and there were puzzles, and news of the child patients who occupied the cot at Great Ormond Street Hospital endowed by readers of *Aunt Judy*.

By the time she took on the magazine Mrs. Gatty's literary career was nearly finished, but she saw in her second daughter, Julie, the writer who was to take over her tradition, and in Mrs. Gatty's own words 'go far beyond me'. She encouraged her generously and enthusiastically, not scrupling to criticize if she felt she could do it constructively, and Julie relied enormously on her mother's opinion. When Julie married and went to live in Canada in 1867 it was a terrible cleavage, felt by both mother and daughter. Mrs. Gatty wrote:

'I feel myself so inferior to Julie, that I *suspect* everyone in the house and out feels the same about it themselves. My hope is, the remembrance of what she would have said, thought, and done, will act upon all of us now she is gone.'

Julie returned from Canada in 1869, and saw a terrible change in her mother, who wrote of herself at this time that

'I cannot walk without labour and risk of stumbling if not falling, and am obliged to *guard* even in walking across the floor of the room. Neither arm has its full power either, and my speech is affected which I think distresses me most of all. At times I feel as if the end of all things in the world must be at hand . . . '

Nevertheless, with the great courage and energy so characteristic of her, she brought out a fifth series of *Parables*, a book of verse, a collection of essays, a book of sundial inscriptions, and one of emblems. After 1871 she could no longer speak or even write, and she spelt out her wishes on a board on which letters were printed. On October 4th, 1873, she died. Julie wrote of her:

'Had she been merely a friend she is one of those whose loss cannot but be felt more as years and experience make one realize the value of certain noble qualities and their rarity . . . She is as much with *me* now as with any of her children even if I am in Jamaica or Ceylon. Now she knows and sees my life, and I have a feeling as if she were an ever-present *conscience* to me . . . which I hope by God's grace may never leave me, and may make me more worthy of having had such a Mother.'

In the November, 1873 issue of *Aunt Judy* Mrs. Ewing wrote a short memoir of her mother, and in the following number appeared 'Madam Liberality' which was inspired by the memory of Mrs. Gatty's unselfishness and generosity. But in Madam Liberality the child she had unconsciously drawn herself when young, always afflicted with some ailment or other (Mrs. Gatty dubbed her the Countess of Homeopathy from the number of times she had to be dosed from the family medicine chest), yet struggling on with an indomitable spirit.

'No sufferings abated her energy for fresh exploits, or quenched the hope that cold, and damp and fatigue would not hurt her "this time".

'In the intervals of wringing out hot flannels for her quinsy she would amuse herself by devising a desert island expedition, on a larger and possibly a damper scale than hitherto, against the time when she should be out again.

'It is a very old simile, but Madam Liberality really was like a cork rising on the top of the very wave of ill-luck that had swallowed up her hopes.

'Her little white face and undaunted spirit bobbed up after each mischance or malady as ready and hopeful as ever.'

Julie was the second eldest of the family, born in 1841. 'A refined little teapot indeed,' wrote her mother lovingly, and at the precocious age of three and a half years she said her Catechism in church with the Sunday School children, and was rewarded with a prayer book. Mrs. Gatty had never really become reconciled to the north and longed for a more congenial climate, but not Julie and her brothers and sisters. To them Ecclesfield and Yorkshire were the only possible places to live, and each of them said so in answer to the question 'In what place would you most like to live?' in the family confession book.

Horatia Katherine Frances Gatty, the third daughter of the family, has left an excellent account of her sister's childhood days in the little book *Juliana Horatia Ewing and her Books* which was published in 1885. Mrs. Ewing's family stories, too, in many cases contain just the same sort of families as the one at Ecclesfield Vicarage, where the children were left largely unsupervised, the elder sisters looking after the younger children, and all of them devoted to dogs, private theatricals, gardening, and playing endless imaginative games. The Gatty boys were given an expensive schooling, but the girls were educated at home, taught by their mother, occasionally by a governess, sometimes, as was the custom of the time, by elder sisters. The girls also worked in the parish (their mother referred to them as doing the work of four curates), decorated the church throughout the year, and practised with the choir. Miss Gatty describes Julie as the promoter of all the nursery doings, and the younger ones relied on her entirely for the organization of every amusement. Especially they demanded to be told stories, and her reputation as a story-teller was such that in an ill-spelt letter from Marlborough her eleven-year-old brother Alfred wrote:

'Do you mind writing me a story when you are well, for I can very seldom get a story book here.'

She invented names for the places they visited on their walks, organized the family theatricals (she usually played a man's part), and edited the family magazines which had a much longer life than most such, with a fairly continuous existence, under different names, for some sixteen years.

In 1861 her first three stories were published in the *Monthly Packet*, to which her mother's connection gave her the entrée: 'A Bit of Green', 'The Blackbird's Nest', and 'Melchior's Dream'. The first two are rather moral little tales with not very much to distinguish them, but the last, a development of the sort of story that her mother wrote, is a very moving allegory, one of the best she ever produced. In 1862 they were published as a book under the title *Melchior's Dream and Other Tales* together with two other stories. Mrs. Gatty wrote an introduction, in which she expressed her sense of privilege at introducing a daughter into the literary world. Privately she recorded her growing discontent with her own writings:

'It makes my child's book drag heavily on my hands, and it is with difficulty I can struggle on to the end. Thankful indeed I shall be when the end comes and *Aunt Judyism* is over! It is impossible to continue it now that the real Aunt Judy has wings, and has soared so far above the imaginary one.'

Julie spent her earnings from this book in a characteristic way. A tenth went to buy some hangings for Ecclesfield Church, and then she took two of her sisters to Whitby for a change of air. After this first book, there was an interval of a couple of years before she settled down to writing again for 'the common cause', as Mrs. Gatty described it; in other words, the Vicarage finances. This may have been the reason she gave for writing at that particular time, but it is perfectly certain that she never needed any incentive to write. Her letters are always full of plans for new stories and books; what her mother found drudgery she found joy. But the story that succeeded 'Melchior's Dream' was uncharacteristic indeed, a Gothicky tale called 'The Mystery of the Bloody Hand', published in the magazine *London Society* in 1865. Her mother seems to have admired it, and to have hoped that Julie was abandoning the writing of children's stories: 'It appears to me that the higher flight suits her best, and is her natural vocation.'

However 'The Mystery of the Bloody Hand' remained an isolated example of 'the higher flight', and the two stories that followed it in the *Monthly Packet* during 1865 were again for children, 'The Yew Lane Ghosts' and 'The Brownies'. By 1866 *Aunt Judy* was founded, and henceforward nearly all her writings were to appear here. She made a beginning with the first two episodes of *Mrs. Overtheway's Remembrances*. But by the time she came to write the third episode she was involved with Alexander Ewing, and the whole family with her.

He wanted to marry her, they opposed him, just as her father had been opposed, and her grandfather before him. He had many characteristics that appealed to the Gattys. He was a devoted member of the Church of England (a cousin of the Bishop of Argyll and the Isles), well-read with a flair for languages, a gifted musician and the composer of a well-known hymn, 'Jerusalem the Golden'—he had in fact studied music in Germany before his family's finances had forced him into an army career. The Gatty opposition seems to have been based on his uncertain future, and perhaps on the usefulness of Julie at home, for the two were admirably suited to each other with exactly the same sort of tastes and eccentricities.

Eventually the family gave way. Julie, who had taken no part in all the tumult of discussion, was in ecstasies, and wrote to a friend:

'He is very clever. A beautiful musician—good linguist—well read, etc.—a dab at meteorology, photography, awfully fond of dogs, good rider, finally a high free mason (a knight Templar) and . . . a mesmerist! Don't laugh at me! I am awfully happy.'

They were married on June 1st, 1867, and a week later sailed for Canada, where Rex Ewing had been posted. Mrs. Gatty wrote:

'I dare not begin to think of how I feel at Julie thus going across the water. But one thing is certain. She could not have been happy *without* him. And her happiness is the only really important point. Children must go *forward* and *outward*, the old folks must be contented that is so.'

II. Mrs Ewing

The 'undaunted spirit' of Madam Liberality remained with Mrs. Ewing throughout her married life, keeping her courageous during eighteen years of the wandering existence of an army wife, four of them being spent without a home of her own, separated from her husband. And her passionate fondness for gardens must have made the nomadic life doubly hard, for any gardener knows that to be forced to leave one's plants is like being torn from one's children. Indeed, her first action as soon as she arrived in new quarters, was to make a garden, no matter how uncompromising the soil and conditions, with the result that, with the fatigue of packing and unpacking, and the frenzy of digging, she was prostrated with the vaguely termed 'bad back' that seems to have dogged her intermittently all her life.

The Victorians suffered a great deal from their backs, especially in novels, but no precise medical details are ever given ('She's the girl with a spine', says one Charlotte Yonge character of another suffering from some unspecified spinal ailment). Ethel Smyth remarked tartly that Mrs. Ewing's letters were 'half-spoiled by constant reference to her poor back, her wretched head, the air-cushion people lent her, the number of hours spent on the sofa after each journey, and so on'. But it was not hypochondria; she was afflicted with very real ill-health all her life, beginning with the severe quinsies that constantly recurred during her childhood. ('Miss Julie were always cayling', a villager at Ecclesfield remarked of her.)

However, in spite of the discomforts an army life brought to a delicate and home-loving woman, it is very likely that marriage made Mrs. Ewing more productive as a writer. This becomes clear if one compares her output before and after 1867. Between 1861 and 1867 she published eleven short stories; between 1867 and 1873 more than twice as many stories and three full-length novels. The unmarried daughters at Ecclesfield Vicarage were used relentlessly as curates and as secretaries; the work on *Aunt Judy* alone was extensive, with Mrs. Gatty hardly able to write and dependent on her daughters. Dr. Gatty also seems to have been a demanding parent;[1] in 1884 he suggested that his youngest daughter should abandon her forthcoming marriage and he his so that they could devote the rest of their lives to each other. It is clear that as long as Julie remained unmarried she would have devoted herself without stint to her parents, particularly her mother, and her writing would have been sacrificed.

As Mrs. Ewing, her life was easier from this point of view, and in between moves, she had plenty of time to write. The first posting, to Canada, lasted two years, and in spite of occasional fierce

[1] A tyrannical one in some respects, perhaps. J. H. E. herself remarked about her sister Undine 'consuming life in the treadmill of running errands for the Governor and slaving at the parish'.

pangs of homesickness, she was very happy. They lived at Fredericton, New Brunswick, in a house they named Reka Dom (the Russian for 'river house'). Mrs. Ewing had first seen this name on a house in Topsham, Devon, and it had delighted her so much that she built the 'Reka Dom' story in *Mrs. Overtheway's Remembrances* round it, and had given the name to their Fredericton house, by the river St. John, in which the story was written.

The letters written home from Canada are full of enthusiastic accounts of her doings, and the delights of sharing them with a husband who was so perfectly of her way of thinking.

Mrs. Ewing spoke of the progress her garden was making, rapturously described the beauties of the white bull-dog that had been added to the household ('I have fallen head over ears in love with another dog. Oh! bless his nose!... His name is Hector'), enthusiastically outlined plans for new stories, told of expeditions to pick mayflowers, and of canoeing leisurely down the river, stopping to sketch or botanize, where the only drawback was that 'the beloved Hector cannot go with us. He would endanger the safety of the canoe.' But in the midst of all these pleasures and a very happy marriage the homesickness would break through overpoweringly, such as when she wrote to her mother in 1869:

'I never had D.'s "spirit" for a wandering life, and it is out of the fullness of my experience that

25

I *know*, and wish unspeakably that I could convey to you, how very much of one's sinking dread has all the *unreality* of fear of an *unknown* evil. . . . I am too much your daughter not to be strongly tempted to "beat my future brow", much more so than to be over-hopeful. Rex is given that way too in his own line . . . Still the natural terrors of an untravelled and not herculean woman about the ups and downs of a wandering, homeless sort of life like ours are not so comprehensible by him, he having travelled so much, never felt a qualm of sea-sickness and less than the average of home-sickness, from circumstances.'

From Canada she contributed to *Aunt Judy* the last two stories in *Mrs. Overtheway's Remembrances*, 'Reka Dom' and 'Kerguelen's Land', and some fairy stories, among them, 'The Land of Lost Toys'. In the autumn of 1869 the Ewings came home, bringing with them an adopted dog of the Newfoundland sort, whom they had named Trouvé, because he had been found locked up in the barracks after the departure of a regiment. There was much joyful weeping in the Vicarage, and a tremendous welcome in Ecclesfield village, and stirred by this, Mrs. Ewing wrote 'Christmas Crackers', a Hans Andersen-like story of a family gathered round the fire at Christmas, the old dreaming of their youth, the young of their future.

Their next posting was to Aldershot, where they were stationed until 1877. Somewhat surprisingly,

26

Mrs. Ewing loved life in an army encampment, and these were by far her most productive years. She liked the climate and the scent of the pines around her, she enjoyed theatricals and concerts and regimental balls, she was even fond of the small military bungalow where they lived, finding it presented a challenge to her powers of making an attractive home. She fully conceded all the disadvantages, and in *The Story of a Short Life* (*Aunt Judy*, 1882) she described how:

'... only the publicity and squalor of the back-premises of the "Lines"—their drying clothes and crumbling mud walls, their coal-boxes and slop-pails—could exceed the depressing effects of the gardens in front, where such plants as were not uprooted by the winds perished of frost and drought, and where, if some gallant creeper had stood fast and covered the nakedness of your wooden hovel, the Royal Engineers would arrive one morning... and tear down the growth of years before you had finished shaving, for the purpose of repainting your outer walls.'

Nevertheless, she was very happy, and became deeply interested in the ordinary soldier. This is apparent not only in *The Story of a Short Life*, but also in the account of the Scottish barracks in *Lob Lie-by-the-fire* (1874), and in *Jackanapes* (*Aunt Judy*, 1879). Long after she left Aldershot she felt nostalgic pangs for it. In *The Story of a*

Short Life she tried to rationalize her love of the place, saying that a military encampment presented life in epitome, the human pilgrimage in brief. But the passage that concludes that chapter more convincingly describes her feeling: the irrational feeling that brings sentimental tears to the eyes of the spectator of the Trooping the Colour ceremony:

'Bare and dusty are the Parade Grounds, but they are thick with memories. Here were blessed the colours that became a young man's shroud that they might not be a nation's shame. Here march and music welcome the coming and speed the parting regiments. On this Parade the rising sun is greeted with gun-fire and trumpet clarions shriller than the cock, and there he sets to a like salute with tuck of drum. Here the young recruit drills, the warrior puts on his medal, the old pensioner steals back to watch them, and the soldiers' children play—sometimes at fighting or flag-wagging, but oftener at funerals!'

Ethel Smyth in *Impressions that Remained* refers to the Ewings' home at Aldershot; the Smyths lived nearby, and Ethel used to visit the Ewings to study music with Rex. The Smyths and the Ewings remained friendly for many years, but Julie and Ethel regarded each other with a certain amount of reserve. Julie admired the latter's musicianship, though she deplored her habit of smoking and her slapdash untidiness, while Dame Ethel implied that Mrs. Ewing fidgeted unnecessarily about her health, and that she seemed to prefer the company of Rex's brother officers to herself.

While she was at Aldershot, Mrs. Ewing wrote three long novels: *A Flat Iron for a Farthing* (*Aunt Judy*, 1870-71), *Six to Sixteen* (*Aunt Judy*, 1872), and *The Miller's Thumb*, later published in book form as *Jan of the Windmill* (*Aunt Judy*, 1872-3). This last novel was begun after a visit to Amesbury in Wiltshire with her husband, and the details of the working of a mill were provided by an old man who having once been a miller, was reduced to selling muffins round the Aldershot camp. But by the time the last episode appeared Mrs. Gatty was dead. After her death, Julie and her sister 'Dot' shared the editorship of *Aunt Judy* for two years, until it was felt that the business side of it was too much for the former, and distracted her from her writing.

Mrs. Ewing was also deeply involved in her own financial transactions, which always seem to have been unsatisfactory. It is hard to understand why she should always have received so little from her publications, even when they were selling in their thousands; when *Jackanapes*, for instance, was selling five hundred a day, she was only receiving a halfpenny royalty on each shilling copy. Besides, in some curious way she used to be heavily involved in the business side of the production of her books, which would lead to exhausting correspondence and large bills to be met before she started to receive any profits. Her publishers were George Bell and Sons, who had also been Mrs. Gatty's publishers (the Gatty family used to refer to the firm as the Tinkler), and Mrs. Ewing wrote bitterly:

'The moment we come to *deal*, the firm's only notion of business is to depreciate and beat me down.'

Randolph Caldecott, who collaborated so successfully with Mrs. Ewing over the illustration of *Lob*, *Jackanapes* and *Daddy Darwin* (the last two of which were published by the S.P.C.K.) was of the opinion that all publishers should be treated as tradesmen:

'I should have no scruple in touching the very bottom of a publisher's coffer. I am sorry to say that I know them a little too well.'

he wrote to Mrs. Ewing when the question of the cost of illustrating *Jackanapes* arose.

Mrs. Ewing had to struggle with all these affairs herself. Major Ewing felt happily that his wife was provided for because of her literary earnings, and on one occasion he even suggested that she should lend him eighty-one pounds to buy a piano, and he would repay her at the rate of fourteen-and-six a week, an arrangement which he had totally forgotten long before the money had been paid back. And the truth was that Mrs. Ewing's literary earnings were very small; in 1883, two years before her death, she wrote that she had that year received not much more than twenty pounds in royalties on ten books. She said sadly:

'I've been nearly twenty years at it, and never got beyond our old groove with nine volumes. Some doing well up to a few thousands, others (like *Lob Lie-by-the-fire*) having brought me in about seven pounds ten shillings in six or seven years!'

In 1877 the happy life at Aldershot came to an end, and the years of wandering began. Major Ewing was posted to Manchester, and went off to search for a house there, while Mrs. Ewing stayed behind to pack. It was the constant packing and unpacking of the next few years, combined with the furious energy that she threw into making a new home, that led, in the opinion of her family, to the deterioration of her health. For a little over a year the Ewings lived at Bowdon, outside Manchester, where Mrs. Ewing began to write *We and the World*, and then Rex was posted to York, and the roots had to be torn up again. Once more, at Fulford, near York, she began to make a new home, having the walls distempered instead of papered, to the consternation of the decorator, the better to show off her pictures. But this only lasted for six months, and then at short notice, Major Ewing was sent to Malta. Mrs. Ewing stayed

31

behind, once more to pack, and also to wait for the cooler autumn weather to travel in.

She spent the next few months visiting friends and relatives, and also enjoying a mild amount of lionizing. She described having her brocade dress rejuvenated for this: 'and the tail of it lined with pale blue—the better to lash with, my dear!' Her bad health caused her to miss much in the way of social occasions, but she did meet Randolph Caldecott, whom she admired enormously, and asked him whether he would consider illustrating a book for her. He agreed, provided they both lived —he himself was dying of heart disease, though he survived Mrs. Ewing by one year.

That same month, June, 1879, the news of the death of the Prince Imperial in the Zulu War moved her deeply, and roused her into writing *Jackanapes*. She took as her text, 'Greater love hath no man than this, that a man lay down his life for his friends.' Miss Gatty gave it as her opinion that:

'if she had still been living at Aldershot, surrounded by the atmosphere of military sympathies and military honour, the tale would never have been written. It was not aimed, as some people supposed, personally at the man who was with the Prince Imperial when he met his death. . . . It was hearing this same man's conduct discussed by civilians from the standard of honour which is unhappily so different in civil and military circles.'

Mrs. Ewing attacked those standards in the person of the Grey Goose, who stands in the background of *Jackanapes* and watches Jackanapes' brief life, baffled and uncomprehending. Jackanapes gives his life to save that of a wounded friend, the life of a young man full of promise given for one who could never make a good officer. The Grey Goose could not understand this, nor could the civilians among whom Mrs. Ewing was living at that time. It was their incomprehension of what constitutes military honour that provoked Mrs. Ewing into writing her book.

Randolph Caldecott provided a picture to illustrate *Jackanapes* when it first appeared in *Aunt Judy* in October, 1879, a picture that had to be drawn, because of the exigencies of colour printing, before the story was ever written. Mrs. Ewing suggested the subject to him, or rather, gave him a choice of subjects, and then wrote the story to fit the drawing he produced—a fair-haired little boy riding a red pony on a village green, and frightening all the geese and the chickens with the trumpet he is blowing. When *Jackanapes* eventually appeared as a book in 1883 with a full set of drawings by Caldecott, this original coloured picture was reproduced much smaller, in black and white.

In October she set out, full of excitement, to join her husband in Malta. She had always been an exceedingly bad traveller, the oscillation of boats, trains and carriages usually brought about complete prostration, and so this route was planned with great care. The heavy luggage was all sent in advance, and she was to travel to Marseilles overland, breaking her journey at Paris. It was a nightmare journey, and by the time she reached Paris she was so ill that she had to wire for help to her youngest sister and a friend, who came out at once and brought her home. The grief of passing through Paris and not being able to see anything of it was very keen, in spite of all her other troubles, and she wrote to her husband:

'You must show your wife Paris! I sobbed myself nearly to bits in the cab as we came away through those lovely streets, and thought of you, and how you love it . . . When we drove past the Louvre and it was open, I was wild to go in and just see Raphael's St. Margaret, but on the whole we daren't risk it, and I collapsed almost directly afterwards.'

Jenner, whom she consulted in London, told her that the pains in her back were due to 'neuralgia of the spine', that she suffered from nervous exhaustion, and in future would do well never to travel without her husband. Once again she was left without a home of her own, in great inconvenience because most of her possessions were now on their way to Malta, and in a certain amount of financial difficulty, for Rex Ewing seems to have been frequently careless about sending off her monthly cheque, which often did not arrive at all, or else was made out for less than his wife had expected. Her friends told her that she was not being fairly dealt with by her publishers, and Ruskin, whom she had met in October, wanted to help her to bring out a volume of her stories independent of any publisher,

'and to mention me in the next *Fors Clavigera* as having joined him in defying the publishing brotherhood. It was an overwhelming temptation to go hand in hand with *him* in anything! But one's safe way in doubt is—to do what is most *right*, and my intercourse with Bell has not been such as to justify me in subscribing to an attack on his honesty.'

Major Ewing came back on special leave in December to see his wife, but she was still not strong enough to travel, and so once more he had to leave her alone, trying to improve her health, and passing the time in visits to friends and relations and Ecclesfield. Her letters to her husband during 1880 are melancholy, in spite of their courage.

'Head and spine very shaky this morning so that I could not get warm; but I wrapped in my fur cloak, and went out into the sunshine, up and down, up and down the churchyard flags. A sunny old kirkyard is a nice place, I always think, for aged folk and invalids to creep up and down in.'

There are also loving descriptions of the Yorkshire country, as though she were trying to fix them in her mind for all eternity.

'Such sweet sunshine, and Greno Wood, with yellow remains of bush and bracken, and heavy mosses on the sandstone walls, and tiny streams trickling through boggy bits of the wood, and coming out over the wall to overflow those picturesque stone troughs which are so oddly numerous and which I had in my head when I wrote the first part of *Mrs. Overtheway*.'

And again to her husband:

'Very dear to me are all your "tender and true" regards for the old home—the grey-green nest (more grey now than green!) a good deal changed and weatherbeaten, but not quite deserted—which is bound up with so much of our lives! . . . Another chord of sympathy was very strongly pulled by your writing of the "grey-green fields", and sending your love to them. No one I ever met has, I think, *quite* your sympathy with exactly what the external world out-of-doors is to me and has been ever since I can remember. From days when the batch of us went-out-walking with the Nurses, and the round moss-edge holes in the roots of gnarled trees in the hedges, and the red leaves of Herb Robert in autumn, and all the inexhaustible wealth of hedges and ditches and fields, and the Shroggs,[1] and the brooks, were happiness of the keenest kind—to now when it is as fresh and strong as ever; it has been a pleasure which has balanced an immense lot of physical pain.'

[1] Shroggs Wood, near Ecclesfield.

Out of this deep feeling for the Yorkshire countryside she wrote *Daddy Darwin's Dovecote* in 1881, in order to give *Aunt Judy's Magazine*, which had passed into the hands of a new publisher, a good start. Under Bell it had been steadily losing money, but David Bogue, who took it over, did not do much better with it. Ruskin, who had a deep admiration for the paper, guaranteed £100 to keep it at the old price of sixpence, but in the August of 1882 the publishers went bankrupt, and again it passed into new hands. It survived three more years, long enough to include a memorial tribute to Mrs. Ewing by Caldecott, and then it finally ceased publication.

Daddy Darwin's Dovecote was the first story Mrs. Ewing had written for some time, for during 1880 she had been too ill to produce anything except two poems. All chance of joining her husband was now at an end, for in May, 1881, he was sent to Ceylon—a climate that her health could never have endured.

In 1881, depressed by the stalemate her literary affairs seemed to have reached, she undertook to write versebooks 'three parts good coloured pictures, one part my verses (these that I have by me) . . . I don't know whether my judgement and sense are worth much in the matter, but I really don't know whom to turn to for better advice, and the verses are *done* and are lying idle.' Twenty-four quarto volumes were issued between 1883-5, illustrated by André, each containing one poem or so.

The verses had previously appeared in *Aunt Judy*, and are not of any great distinction, though they were quite popular at the time.

In 1882 her health improved a little, and letters are written from London, Amesbury, and Aldershot—the last two places rousing great nostalgia. This year too *Laetus Sorte Mea, or, The Story of a Short Life* appeared in *Aunt Judy*, and Mrs. Ewing wrote proudly in October of 'two young barristers who have been reading it aloud to each other in the Temple—with tears'. In November she wrote to a friend:

'Rex is to come home in Spring!—the season of hope and *nest-building*—and I am trying not to wonder my wits away as to what part of the British Isles it will be in which I shall lay the cross-sticks and put in the moss and wool of our next nest!'

In great excitement she began again buying pictures and furniture for the new home. Her melancholy left her, she even helped with some theatricals at Shoeburyness and took two parts. By June, 1883, Rex was home and they were settled at the Villa Ponente, outside Taunton. She loved the house, and busied herself with making a garden, digging it herself, and begging plants off friends. Her last works dealt with gardens, *Mary's Meadow* (*Aunt Judy*, 1883-4) and 'Letters from a Little Garden'(*Aunt Judy*, 1884-5). Throughout 1884 her letters are full of the news of her garden, though towards the end there are references to neuralgia, seemingly not taken very seriously: 'Rex says I brought my afflictions on myself by writing too prolix letters several hours a day.' In January, 1885, she still wrote of neuralgia:

'I have not been very well for some time more than yourself, and I am afraid the root of this break-down has been overwork. But the weather has been very sunless and wretched, and I have had a fortnight in bed with bad, periodic neuralgia, which has particularly disabled my right arm and head.'

Even in February, though she was in constant pain, nobody seemed to take a very grave view of her illness, and she talked confidently of feeling better, and visiting Aldershot in a few weeks. It was thought that a change of air might do her good, and she was taken to Bath, but after two days she was again in bed. She lay there, watching the birds building nests in the ivy-covered wall she could see through her window, and laughing over *Huckleberry Finn* as it was read aloud to her. She endured two operations (presumably for the removal of a growth from the spine),[1] and died the

[1]The imprecision of medical detail in the 19th century, the vagueness of the descriptions, make it often very difficult to know the cause of death. In Mrs. Ewing's case, her sister and biographer never states it. She says that J.H.E., early in February, 1885, 'was found to be suffering from a species of blood poisoning'. Mrs. Maxwell, their niece, in her biography, specifically mentions cancer. One can only therefore infer the nature of the operations of 1885.

day after the second, the eve of the Ascension, May 13th, 1885. Miss Gatty wrote of her death:

'Perhaps it is well for us all to know that she found, as others do, the intervals of exhausted relief between attacks of pain were not times in which (had it been needed) she could have changed her whole character, and, what is called, "prepared to die". Our days of health and strength are the ones in which this preparation must be made, but for those who live, as she did, with their whole talents dedicated to God's service, death is only the gate of life—the path from joyful work in this world to greater capacities and opportunities for it in the other.'

She was buried in Trull churchyard, near Bath, her coffin carried by the sergeant-major and staff sergeants of the 13th Regimental District. And in Ecclesfield church there are two stained-glass windows, one to the memory of Mrs. Gatty, the other to Mrs. Ewing.

III. Mrs Ewing and her Contemporaries

The dominant influence on Mrs. Ewing's writing was undoubtedly her mother; as Mrs. Gatty had written allegories and family stories, so Mrs. Ewing continued in the genre. But whereas Mrs. Gatty had had to rely on the real happenings at Ecclesfield Vicarage to supply the little anecdotes in *Aunt Judy's Tales* and *Aunt Judy's Letters*, Mrs. Ewing with her greater powers of imagination could invent her children, and develop their doings into whole novels.

Although Mrs. Ewing took over her mother's themes, fashion had changed by the time she came to write, and a greater humanity towards children is evident in all her writing. Mrs. Gatty did not belong to the generation that held children must be reformed with every word that was written for them, nor would she have shared Mrs. Sherwood's conception of the parent as omniscient and god-like ('I stand in the place of God to you' says Mr. Fairchild to his son Henry, 'whilst you are a child'). But her attitude to children was didactic, she felt that she should underline the moral that each story contained, and, like other writers of her generation, Charlotte Yonge, for instance, she did place heavy moral responsibilities on the child and expect a submission to the Divine Will which it is very unlikely a child could achieve. In the story 'Rabbits' Tails', the children in the introductory paragraphs clamour for a story from the eldest sister, who has been ill, and one little sister says, 'If you were not to get better, I shouldn't want to get better either.'

But she is rebuked:

'Think what poor ignorant infants we all are in the hands of God, not knowing what is either good or bad for us; and then you will see how glad and thankful you ought to be, to be chosen for by somebody wiser than yourself. We must always be contented with God's choice about whatever happens.'

In the hands of Mrs. Gatty the allegory was a little homily illustrated either by day to day occurrences (by the sight of her children watching the motes dance in a sunbeam, for instance), or by the example of the robin, the dragonfly larva, the house cricket. The habits of these creatures were observed with scientific exactitude, and she wrote of Kingsley's *Water Babies*, which she admired although she worried a little because she could not work out an allegorical basis:

'I think my dragon flies better than his and more strictly correct. He makes them split under the water and walk up the stem after.'

But scientific exactness hardly makes for a good story in itself, and the *Parables from Nature* seem somewhat heavy and plodding.

42

Mrs. Ewing also wrote allegories inspired by nature, 'The Blind Hermit and the Trinity Flower', 'Dandelion Clocks', 'Ladders to Heaven', but in each case the flower suggested a story, and the story is powerful enough for the child not to be overwhelmed by the moral, while the more sophisticated reader can be moved by the allegory and the subtlety of the telling. 'The Blind Hermit and the Trinity Flower' (originally published in the *Monthly Packet* in 1871) was preferred by Charlotte Yonge to anything Mrs. Ewing had then written, and is the story of a hermit who spends his life growing herbs to heal the sick, until he becomes blind and can no longer continue. He cannot accept the loss of his sight without bitterness, and prays every day for a cure. At last in a vision he is told of a herb called the Trinity Flower that will cure him, and the root of the plant is sent to him by an angel messenger. His serving boy plants it, and eagerly awaits the spring for it to flower. As it grows the hermit becomes more reconciled to his affliction: 'and, when the boy oftimes repeated, "Thou shalt yet see," the Hermit answered, "If God will. When God will. As God will".' And the night that the flower opens the Hermit dies. As Miss Gatty says of this story in her short biography: 'He who once was blind sees, but his vision is opened on eternal Day.' This illustration of the acceptance of God's will shows the imagination that Mrs. Gatty lacked, and a humanity that makes the elder sister's little lecture in 'Rabbits' Tails' seem harsh indeed.

In 'Dandelion Clocks' Mrs. Ewing tries to convey the passing of time, how it goes slowly for some, quickly for others, but old age inevitably comes and brings behind it a new generation to blow at the dandelions and wonder what time is. 'Ladders to Heaven', the old-fashioned name for lilies of the valley, describes how flowers can be used to clothe the scars made by industry. But the story which developed Mrs. Gatty's allegories to their furthest, and is an example of the new frivolity that had come into children's books with *Alice's Adventures in Wonderland* in 1865, is 'Snap-Dragons' (*Monthly Packet*, 1870). It deals with the Skratdj family, who seldom seriously quarrelled, but they never agreed about anything.

' . . . it was the bystanders who had the worst of it on these occasions. To the worthy couple themselves the habit had become second nature, and in no way affected the friendly tenor of their domestic relations. They would interfere with each other's conversation, contradicting assertions, and disputing conclusions for a whole evening; and then when all the world and his wife thought that these ceaseless sparks of bickering must blaze up into a flaming quarrel as soon as they were alone, they would bowl amicably home in a cab, criticizing the friends who were commenting upon them.'

This flippancy, and the assumption that adults can be criticized as freely as children, makes a sharp contrast with the earlier Victorian writers, especially as in the end it is only the Skratdj children who are cured of their snapping habits, after Harry Skratdj has been made to dance with the Snap-Dragons:

'I doubt if the parents ever were cured. I don't know if they heard the story. Besides, bad habits are not easily cured when one is old.'

Charlotte Yonge, who began writing in 1844 and published her last two novels in 1900, recognized the change that had come about the attitude of the young towards their elders since her youth, and in *Beechcroft at Rockstone* (1889), in which she valiantly but rather unsuccessfully tried to write about the modern girl of the late 'eighties, she makes Lady Merrifield remark sadly:

'I think the difference was that no faults of the elders were dwelt upon by a loyal temper. To find fault was thought so wrong that the defects were scarcely seen, and were concealed from ourselves as well as others. It would scarcely, I suppose, be possible to go back to that unquestioning state, now the temper of the times is changed; but I belong enough to the older days to believe that the true safety is in submission in the spirit as well as the letter.'

Charlotte Yonge was the supreme supporter of parental authority, and though few of her contemporaries carried it quite to the lengths she was prepared to go to (she herself, having been forbidden as a young girl by her mother to go into cottagers' houses, honoured this ruling till her own death, in spite of all the difficulties that it made in her work with the parish schools), the attitude of the child in the pre-1860 novel towards its parents and elders was, in general, awe and devotion, and a sense of the absolute rightness of their judgement in all matters.

In her approach to authority, Mrs. Ewing strikes a modern note; her attitude is much more in line with the feeling of the twentieth century than with her predecessors. Of course she was not the initiator; Catherine Sinclair had introduced a note of levity among the grown-ups in *Holiday House* as early as 1839, and Kingsley in *The Water Babies* (1863) tended to ally himself with the children against the grown-up world, though in rather an arch and fatiguing manner. But Mrs. Ewing's real achievement was in representing the adults as fallible human beings whilst striking a perfect balance between treating the children as hopelessly contaminated with original sin, or else as angels of light, doomed to die young. She also avoided the later, more mawkish version of the second, which probably began with Florence Montgomery's *Misunderstood* in 1869, where the child is in the right and his elders are in the wrong

46

because they simply fail to understand him. Amy le Feuvre took up the theme, so did Frances Hodgson Burnett with *The Little Princess*—Sara Crewe putting her teachers to shame with her high-bred manners and her flawless French accent may be every child's favourite daydream, but she is as unrealistic as the heroes and heroines of *Ministering Children*. In a situation of the same sort, Miss Mulberry's school in Mrs. Ewing's *Six to Sixteen*, where the girls are homesick, too rigidly super-vised, badly fed, their health neglected, Mrs. Ewing concedes that it was not a good school, but that the authorities acted with good motives; there are no emotional orgies of pity for the children concerned.

A religious background is implicit in very nearly all nineteenth-century children's stories, though in general the emphasis grows less, until by the 'nineties or thereabouts the idea that children should be educated in religious matters from their reading, has given way to books written primarily to entertain. Mrs. Molesworth's children go to church on Sundays but we are given no indication of their religious feelings, whereas in the earlier half of the century we would be left in no doubt. Mrs. Ewing's religious faith pervaded all that she wrote, but she did not write sermons, her children did not experience sudden conversions, or reform their elders. There is a background in all her books of simple, practical piety, of church both morning and afternoon on Sunday, of good works done as

47

unobtrusively as possible. The picture of the parson's daughter at the beginning of *Daddy Darwin's Dovecote* is the perfect example of Mrs. Ewing's conception of how one's religious duties should be performed. It is a short chapter, well under a thousand words, describing Saturday night in the Vicarage, and the Vicar's daughter's self-imposed duties, but in it Mrs. Ewing reveals her own religious practice. She had not the intense inner life of someone like Charlotte Yonge, and one does not get the impression that any of her characters would spend much time in sustained religious thought; they were people of action. So, her parson's daughter devotes Saturday evening to balancing the parish money bags, during which a tenth is taken from her dress and pocket money allowances and put into the charity bag, and she takes the decision to devote the latter to buying small extras for the treat she is giving the work-house children to celebrate her twenty-first birthday. In this Mrs. Ewing was exactly describing her own practices. Then she:

'set about the rest of her Saturday night's duties without further delay.

'She put out her Sunday clothes, and her Bible and Prayer-book, and class-book and pencil, on the oak chest at the foot of the bed. She brushed and combed the silver-haired terrier, who looked abjectly depressed whilst this was doing, and preposterously proud when it was done. She washed her own hair, and studied her Sunday-school lesson for the morrow whilst it was drying.

'Then she went to bed, and slept as one ought to sleep on Saturday night, who is bound to be at the Sunday School by 9-15 on the following morning, with a clear mind on the Rudiments of the Faith, the History of the Prophet Elisha, and the destination of each of the parish magazines.'

Mrs. Ewing was markedly free from the almost fanatical Sabbatarianism that was such a feature of all levels of churchmanship in the Victorian period, and which strove to apply the rules of the Jewish Sabbath to the Christian Sunday. It was present in the stern, evangelical low church books of A.L.O.E. (A Lady of England—Charlotte Mary Tucker) who in *The Children's Tabernacle* (1871) describes the fearful mental torment of the little girl who sews a curtain on a Sunday for the model of the Israelite Tabernacle which she and her brothers and sisters are making to entertain a Ragged School, and equally present in Charlotte Yonge's novels, for all her Tractarian affiliations and hatred of puritanism. Very nearly the only reference to the rigid Sunday code of Mrs. Ewing's contemporaries comes in *A Flat Iron for a Farthing*, where Regie is tempted into tree-climbing on a Sunday by his high-spirited cousin who, to excuse this rather wild behaviour, pretends that the tree is a church and she is the preacher. Nurse Bundle comes out and scolds the children, but nobody thinks very much of the incident. Otherwise, as long as there is the customary morning and afternoon attendance at church, there seem to be few restrictions on the children, and Jack in *We and the World* goes off on a Sunday for a picnic on the moors with the bee-keeper, carrying his sandwiches in a red and orange spotted handkerchief slung on the end of a stick (' "And they'll just meet the Ebenezer folk coming out of chapel, ma'am!" said our housemaid over my mother's shoulder, by way of consolation.')

There is no doubt that Mrs. Ewing's rule of reticence aided her in an age which has perhaps never been equalled for the lavish way its emotions were expended in public, private, and in fiction Mrs. Ewing wrote of this rule, that

'young writers of talent break almost invariably. No class of literature is a more striking example of the blunder of throwing away powder and shot than tracts—and I sometimes wonder if any recognized form of literature has more in its power. It is almost next to drama for what it has to work upon, the highest hopes, the deepest sufferings of humanity . . . and a real artist needs strong warrants of Conscience when he dips into those primary colours. In a fit of enthusiasm Ruskin wanted to lay a tax on all colours but Black, Prussian blue, Vandyke brown, and Chinese white. I suspect it would be greatly to the advantage of *our* Art if to depict some of the deeper emotions and experiences of Humanity were forbidden . . .

till years of discretion. "Make your *white* precious" is a quaint saying of Ruskin's which I often recall when I write.'

She was perhaps thinking of Hesba Stretton, the author of *Jessica's First Prayer* (1867), Mrs. O. F. Walton (*Christie's Old Organ*, 1883), Brenda (*Froggie's Little Brother* 1879), and the lush and emotional stories issued in such large numbers by the Religious Tract Society, that Eliza Keary described disapprovingly as those 'sensational stories of ragged London depravity, which do duty as Sunday books nowadays'. Nearly all of them contained a deathbed scene, often the premature death of a child, with affecting details of the last words he speaks to those around him. Mrs. Ewing herself seems to guy this in *A Flat Iron for a Farthing*, when Regie catches fever:

'As I wished, the rector prayed by my bedside; and I think he must have been rather astonished by the fact that at points which struck me I rather groaned than said, "Amen". The truth is, I had once happened to go into a cottage where our old rector was praying by the bed of a sick old man—a Methodist —who groaned "Amen" at certain points in a manner which greatly impressed me, and I now did likewise, in that imitativeness of childhood which had helped to lead me to the fancy for surrounding my own sick bed with all the circumstances I had seen or heard of in such cases in the village

51

'... I begged (Nurse Bundle) would not fail to cover up all the furniture with white cloths, and to allow all my friends to come and see me in my coffin.'

But even Mrs. Ewing was not above the desire to make her readers weep, and was apt to write enthusiastically to her family of passages from her latest story that she thought would bring tears. This was not necessarily achieved by a death, it might be the reunion of Ida with her father in *Mrs. Overtheway's Remembrances*, or the departure of the magic shoes, signifying the end of a childhood, in 'Timothy's Shoes', and only in one book, in most ways quite uncharacteristic of her, did she base her whole story on the death of a child. This is *Laetus Sorte Mea, or, The Story of a Short Life* (*Aunt Judy*, 1882).

It was received by her contemporaries with great enthusiasm, and in some ways it has much merit. The descriptions of Aldershot, written out of Mrs. Ewing's nostalgia for her former home, are excellent; so is the evocation of the better aspects of Army life, and her warm account of the common soldier, who had until then never received such sympathetic treatment from a novelist. But Mrs. Ewing was always at her best when she was writing about the things she knew, and in this case she had chosen a subject quite outside her experience— the lingering illness and death of a young child.

The deathbed was of course a convention in

Victorian novels, and probably many of the writers who used it were aware that their descriptions bore very little resemblance to fact. Hesba Stretton, for instance, wrote to edify and convert, and seems not to have cared particularly about accuracy in achieving these ends. But Mrs. Ewing did care very deeply about accuracy; before she wrote *A Great Emergency* she wanted to undertake a barge journey down a canal to check the details of the route; *Jan of the Windmill* was not written until she had thoroughly steeped herself in the Wiltshire dialect and the workings of a mill. So the illness and the death of Leonard in *The Story of a Short Life*, being written entirely from her imagination, lack the conviction of all her other books. He falls from a carriage at a military review, and spends the rest of his short life (he is only six) in much suffering from a spinal injury which is never defined. Finally he is dying, and at his urgent request he is taken to the army encampment that he loves, to die a soldier's death. It has been stated with some medical authority that in fact people very rarely know how near they are to death, that it is left to relations and nurses to send for the clergy. Thus it is inconceivable that a child of six within a few minutes of his death should have the physical strength and clearness of mind to say, in a long speech, that he hoped he would not die until he had heard just one more verse of his favourite hymn which was being sung at that moment in the nearby encampment chapel.

It is a tribute to Mrs. Ewing's powers as a writer that one can criticize an unlikely episode in this manner, for the plot of the average story at that time was a network of implausibility and fantastic coincidence, with very little attention paid to psychological probability. But Mrs. Ewing's work is so much better than these, so carefully considered, that it must be judged by higher standards. Deaths occur in her other stories, indeed, it is rarely absent from her longer books, but she gave her reason for this in the short story 'Three Christmas Trees':

'Of course he died at last. The best and happiest of men must die; and it is only because some stories stop short in their history, that every hero is not duly buried before we lay down the book.'

Her sister Horatia ('Dot') records that, inspired by a picture at a London exhibition, Mrs. Ewing stayed awake that night planning a story to be built around it and a quotation from Thomas à Kempis that she thought summarized the picture: 'Respice finem—in all things, remember the end'. The story never got written, but this sentiment dominated her writing, it inspired many of her short stories, and in her longer books it led her to account for her characters until the end of their lives.

The only other occasion when the plot of one of her stories owed much to the conventions of the times was in very nearly her best book, *Jan of the*

Windmill. It hinges on the mystery of Jan's parentage—concealed relationship was a topic as much loved by the later Victorian children's writers as hidden treasure is today—and there is also a child-stealing, another common theme, though in this case it is a huckster who steals Jan, not the usual gipsy. But in the first part of the book we are hardly aware that the plot is not original, so skilfully does Mrs. Ewing manipulate it. On a wild night of storm, the wife of Abel Lake the miller is lamenting her youngest child who has just died because the hard-headed miller has refused to call a doctor. As the thunder rolls round the mill, and Abel Lake struggles to reef the mill's sails, two strangers arrive, and ask whether he will consider taking as a foster-child the baby they have brought with them, no questions to be asked, but ten shillings a week to be paid for his keep. The child Jan is brought up as the Lake's own son, but from the very first shows himself different from the miller's tow-headed offspring. He is black-eyed, alert, and intelligent, and he loves drawing. Little Abel, the miller's eldest child, nurses and tends the baby Jan with a charming devotion, and the miller's man, George, watches on, hiding a cunning malevolence under the expression of a simpleton. He is certain there is a mystery about Jan's parentage, and he wants to make money out of it.

This part of the story comes near to greatness. There is a wonderful feeling of the wide spaces of Salisbury Plain, with the clouds soaring overhead;

of the mill, the chains jangling as the sacks of grist go up to be ground, the sound of the wind roaring in the round-house and the millstones overhead flying round and shaking the roof. There is also a masterly tension and drama, and a sense of brooding evil, as the miller's man watches the boy, and the Cheap Jack, the villain of the book, plots to use the former as a tool.

Mrs. Ewing's difficulty arises, as it was apt to in her longer works, when she comes to relate childhood to subsequent events. She wants to make Jan into a great artist, and restore him to his own father. Her account of his beginnings is very convincing; first he draws pigs on his slate as he yawns over his lessons, then, when he is set to minding a neighbour's pigs, he paints landscapes on the ground with leaves and twigs. A little girl gives him a paintbox, and from the experience he gets in using this, he paints a sign for the local innkeeper. But this has absorbed two-thirds of the book, and there is much to be told yet. So Jan is kidnapped by the Cheap Jack and taken to London where he is forced to draw on pavements to make money. He runs away, finds shelter in a boys' home, and there is discovered by a visiting artist in search of a model. He learns the craft, and a painting of him by his master is seen by his true father in an exhibition, the mystery about his parentage is cleared up, he marries an heiress (the little girl who gave him the paintbox), and returns to the district of his childhood as the squire and a painter of great reputation. Mrs. Ewing was doubly successful in the first part of the book, in the picture of the mill and the miller's family, where her sense of atmosphere and her characterization are really distinguished, and in the account of the beginnings of a great painter. She failed when she took Jan away from the mill, partly because she was only on sure ground when she dealt with country matters.

It is Mrs. Ewing's country books that are her unique contribution to children's literature: *Daddy Darwin's Dovecote*, *Lob Lie-by-the-fire*, *Jackanapes* and *Jan of the Windmill*. Plenty of books had been written about the country before but the convention of the times was that there were two entirely different reading publics for children's books, the educated and the uneducated, and that neither cared to read about the other. Charlotte Yonge herself wrote for both: what she termed 'drawing-room stories' for the upper and middle classes, and shorter books about cottage children for the boys and girls she taught in the parish schools at Otterbourne. At this time the only books that were written about village life were specifically intended for the cottager's child, and were usually designed to point a simple moral—that practical jokes were silly and dangerous, that young children should not be left alone with fires, of the terrible consequences of not telling the truth, and so when Charlotte Yonge came to fit *Daddy Darwin's Dovecote* and the other country books into the pattern of her pamphlet of 1887, *What Books to Lend and What to Give*, which was chiefly intended for parish schools, but did also have a section of 'drawing-room stories', she was in rather a dilemma. By their subject matter she felt they were best suited for country children, but, she wrote:

'These exquisite pieces are too delicately worked for the ordinary style of children of the poor, though they may be appreciated by those who have time to dream over them, and, as it were, imbibe them.'

She included them eventually in 'drawing-room stories', but put *Jackanapes* in the section for boys' schools, adding a rider that 'those who read it to them find it advisable to skip the unnecessary incident of the elopement'.

One can be tolerably certain that, like all the best children's books, these were not written for any specific type of reader but to please the author herself. She embodied in them her intense love and sympathy for the country and country people, and in *Daddy Darwin's Dovecote*, perhaps the best of all her works, her devotion to that part of Yorkshire in which she had been born. She was in bad health at the time, her husband was stationed abroad, she had no home of her own, and perhaps to put these harsh realities behind her, she described the places she had known so well as a child, and had longed for in her homesickness in Canada—Shroggs Wood, Grenoside, and their neighbourhood.

It is a short book with a simple story, told with the great economy characteristic of her shorter works. She had laid down rules for her writing, founded on principles of drawing, and indeed very much influenced by Ruskin's *Elements of Drawing*, saying that 'the whole *dramatis personae* should be settled upon and arranged into classes, those for the foreground, those for the middle distance, those for the background'. But only in her short works does she seem to adhere completely to this axiom, partly because when she involved herself with a large set of characters she became fond of them and wanted to follow their fortunes throughout their lives. In *Daddy Darwin* there are only two main characters, Daddy Darwin, the grumbling, suspicious, lonely old man, and Jack March the foundling who ends by inheriting the dovecote and the smallholding. The book opens with a preamble, two gaffers gossiping as they sit on a wall, discussing a young man who is passing. In the following pages the brief history of that young man and Daddy Darwin is told, and how it has come about that from starting life in the workhouse, Jack March has become the owner of Darwin's Dovecote. Mrs. Ewing uses just two or three incidents to sketch in the passing of twenty odd years. She begins with little Jack March resting from his toil in the workhouse garden and watching with envious eyes the glorious freedom of the pigeons flying home to Darwin's Dovecote, and the letter he writes to Daddy Darwin asking to be allowed

59

to mind his pigeons. The central incident, round which the book is built, is the theft of the pigeons and their recovery by Jack March. After that his position is secure, and when Daddy Darwin dies some years later, the workhouse boy inherits the property.

'The gaffer's tale is told. "Craw! Craw! Craw!" The crows flapped slowly home, and the Gaffers moved off too. The sun was down, and "damps" are bad for "rheumatics".'

There is no tension in this story, nor surprise. Its great merit lies in the skill and the economy of the telling of it, the vividness of the Yorkshire community and the account of the village life, for in her background Mrs. Ewing sketched in a whole range of characters from the parson's daughter, to Phoebe Shaw, the 'neatest woman in the parish'. Mrs. Ewing herself referred to this book as 'my best and tersest and most finished writing'.

Lob Lie-by-the-fire is also the story of a foundling, though one not so satisfactory as Jack March. Into a world reminiscent of *Cranford* comes a small gipsy baby that Miss Kitty and Miss Betty of Lingborough Hall find by the road on their way home from taking tea with 'the widow of General Dunmaw'. Against all advice they adopt him and give him the name of John Broom. But he grows up idle and a wanderer, and finally, at the age of twelve or so, he runs away to sea. It takes many years and much wandering before he returns to Lingborough again, and even when he does, he is so ashamed of his former reputation and the years that have passed that he does not know how to introduce himself. So he plays the part of the house-elf, Lob Lie-by-the-fire, who does the work while everybody is asleep. When he is at last found out he settles down at Lingborough for the rest of his life.

Plenty of books were being written at this time for village children about the ne'er-do-well boy who makes good, but most of them crude, extreme in the blackness and whiteness of their characters, lacking in any literary interest. It is startling to find what a promising subject it is in the hands of a writer as accomplished as Mrs. Ewing. Again she took immense trouble with her background, in this case the small gentry of a Border town, and she drew them with a care and a subtlety which is far beyond what a child reader would expect or would appreciate: the charities of Miss Betty and Miss Kitty, hidden from each other; the tea-parties of their small circle where 'supper was served at nine, and the parson and the lawyer played whist for love with different partners on different evenings with strict impartiality'; the sarcastic lawyer who so unnerved Miss Kitty at these gatherings by his 'dexterity in suggesting doubts of everything', while she valiantly

'fought for Church and State, for parsons and poor people, for the sincerity of her friends, the virtues of the Royal Family, the merit of Dr. Drugson's prescriptions, and for her favourite theory that there is some good in every one and some happiness to be found everywhere'.

And all the time that John Broom is away from Lingborough, homeless and wandering, lacking the courage to return, Mrs. Ewing skilfully suggests the home in the background, where everything stays much as it always has done, except that time passes and everybody gets a little older. Thus, when we return to Lingborough after John Broom's long travels, the servants at the Hall are the same ones, only a little more idle and careless, and there is still the same circle taking tea with Mrs. General Dunmaw, though the sceptical lawyer is now married and not quite so sarcastic.

Jackanapes, probably the best known book of the three, and certainly the favourite of Mrs. Ewing's contemporaries, has all the same skill that went into the other two, but has survived the years less well. It belongs to a time when England was a great power, and wars and the military life could still be considered glorious. Reading it some eighty years later, it is not the battle scenes that stir and move the reader, but the account of country life at the beginning and end of the book, and the truth that seems to emerge from it is that it is the places like Goose Green that have permanence and substance, and people like the Grey Goose (in whom Mrs. Ewing was castigating the civilian and 'commercial' sense of honour as against the military code) who have the most sense.

Goose Green is the background of the story, and the people who live on it form the background characters—the Grey Goose, the donkeys, Miss Jessamine (Jackanapes' aunt), the Postman. They are, so as to speak, the chorus. The Grey Goose sees Jackanapes learn to walk, ride his first horse (on a roundabout), become the owner of Lollo, his first pony.

'Twenty odd years later the Grey Goose was still alive, and in full possession of her faculties, such as they were. She lived slowly and carefully, and she lived long.'

But Jackanapes had gone off to war. There is a brief picture of the engagement in which he is fatally wounded, saving the life of Tony Johnson, his greatest friend from the Goose Green years, and his death in a hospital tent. And then we are back in Goose Green. Lollo the pony, very old now, pulls Miss Jessamine in her bath chair, Captain Johnson walks beside them, the Grey Goose watches.

'The sun, setting gently to his rest, embroiders the sombre foliage of the oak-tree with threads of gold. The Grey Goose is sensible of an atmosphere of repose, and puts up one leg for the night. The grass glows with a more vivid green, and, in answer to a ringing call from Tony, his sisters, fluttering over the daisies in pale-hued muslins, come out of their ever-open door, like pretty pigeons from a dovecote.

'And if the good gossips' eyes do not deceive them, all the Miss Johnsons, and both the officers, go wandering off into the lanes, where bryony wreaths still twine about the brambles.'

These three books stand quite apart from anything else the ninteenth century accomplished in children's literature. It is, however, interesting to read Mrs. Gatty's short story 'The Hundredth Birthday' in the light of what Mrs. Ewing achieved later in her pictures of country life. 'The Hundreth Birthday' is an account of a village community where an old woman becomes more and more certain that on her hundredth birthday she is going to dine with the Queen. As a study of old age, its mingled childishness and sagacity, and in Mrs. Gatty's deep understanding of the country character, it is equal to *Daddy Darwin's Dovecote*. It also contains a moving and convincing account of the death of a very old woman—and deathbeds are the weakest part of many Victorian stories, even of some of Mrs. Ewing's. But the fashion of the time in which Mrs. Gatty was writing made her round off 'The Hundredth Birthday' with a little sermon about the nature of the supernatural, which spoils the subtlety of what had gone before. Mrs. Ewing, writing later, was able to leave her moral to be inferred.

IV. The Writer of Family Stories and Magic

Family stories have always held a very large place in English children's literature. Far more than plot, their readers demand characters that they can develop an affection for, and an abundance of domestic incident. But by their very nature such stories are apt to date and lose interest for future generations—a too accurate reflection of the age and society in which the writer lived may bore later children. Thus it has been with Charlotte Yonge, whose May, Merrifield, Mohun, and Underwood chronicles so delighted mid-Victorian children. She still has her elderly and middle-aged admirers now, but this side of her work could never be revived to any great extent for children of today. The children who may not jump off a stone because it is Sunday, the adolescents who worry about the consequences of delayed confirmation in the case of sudden death, the girl who gives up a walk with her sisters and the governess on the grounds of propriety because a young male visitor decides to accompany them—these belong to an infinitely remote society, where the remoteness has not even the quality of romance.

From all this Mrs. Ewing escapes. She is not typically 'Victorian', though perhaps the conception of what is typically Victorian is too often based on the Charlotte Yonge proprieties. Mrs. Ewing's children belong to every age; their interests do not date them—dressing-up, and dogs, and gardens are as popular as ever they were—nor do their emotions. In 'Our Field', for instance, a short story so greatly admired by Ruskin that he called it a poem, not a story, she manages to convey that blissful losing of oneself in play, that satiation with happiness and complete unawareness of future trouble, which it is impossible to find after the age of ten or so. She records, too, the craving that all children know—for a place of their own: 'No matter where we made our home, it was sure to be disturbed.' But one of the boys finds a field, and there the children play all summer, uninterrupted. The field has everything, a brook with fresh-water shrimps; bluebells, cowslips, a hollow oak, and they accept it, untroubled by thoughts of its ownership, by all the possibilities that would spoil an adult pleasure—that they may be turned off, that the field may be ploughed up, built upon.

Mrs. Ewing's preoccupation with country matters has been in her favour too. In an urban civilisation it is still the country that provides the setting for most children's books. Children are escapists; it takes an adult degree of sophistication to find interest in wet pavements and rows of grimy terraced houses. However little experience they have of country matters children will still accept books that deal with aspects of it in some technical detail—riding, sailing, farming. *Mary's Meadow* for all its talk of gardening matters, can absorb a town child in its account of how Mary, Arthur, Harry, Adela, and Christopher take plants and cuttings from their gardens and set them in waste-places, and hedges and fields. This book so stirred its readers at the time that a Parkinson Society was formed to do precisely that, and Mrs. Ewing was its first president. (It was Parkinson's herbal that inspired the children in the book to play this game.)

But the greatest of all Mrs. Ewing's merits for the modern reader is the emancipation of the child from the adult world and adult moral reponsibilities that had dragged him down in the pre-1860 books. The adults in children's books have always presented the author with a problem, and the common twentieth-century technique of making the children seem to exist in an adult-less vacuum (Arthur Ransome's holiday books, for instance) is rather an artificial solution, remote from what usually happens in real life. Mrs. Ewing puts her children against a background of adults, but she treats her readers as equals, and freely makes fun of the adult's behaviour.

Her three longest family stories, *A Flat Iron for a Farthing*, *Six to Sixteen*, and *We and the World* are outstanding from this point of view, and as they are all written in the form of memoirs, the narrators, being supposedly grown up by the time of writing, are able to give a detached account of their parents' personalities, which a child, who accepts his parents uncritically, would be unable to do. Thus Jack in *We and the World* can say:

'Few things are harder to guess at than the grounds on which an Englishman of my father's type makes up his mind.'

And of his mother: 'She was timid and vacillating from wifely habit.' *We and the World* is in some ways the most interesting book of the three. It is a very perceptive study of a boy's character and childhood, and in none of Mrs. Ewing's books is the Yorkshire background depicted more evocatively. But the plot got out of hand (the book was written at a time of much packing and moving house), and Part I had reached the dimensions of a full-length book, with still the main part of the story to be told —her hero leaving home and going out into the world. The account of his life at sea is a remarkable *tour de force* for a woman who was drawing on her imagination and what she had gleaned from more knowledgeable friends, but for all her affection for them, the characters of Alister and Dennis, Jack's two friends, do not carry much conviction. and this part of the book becomes almost tedious, a fault she had never before fallen into.

A Flat Iron for a Farthing contains some of her best characters—the strong-minded Aunt Maria and the girl cousins; Nurse Bundle; the cousins' governess whose 'peculiarities were conscientiousness and the fidgets, and tendencies to fine crochet, calomel, and Calvinism, and an abiding quality of harassing and being harassed'; Regie's tutor, and the two dogs, Rubens and Sweep. The book takes

Reginald Dacre from babyhood to marriage, but is principally concerned with him up to the age of twelve. The incident that links the child with the young man is the one that gives the book its title. As a small boy he sees two little girls buying a farthing flat iron at a village shop. Not for some years does he discover who they are, and then it seems that they are dead. But the story ends with their reappearance, and Regie falls as deeply in love with the younger one as he did when he first saw her in the Oakford ironmonger's shop. The fortunes of all the characters are followed up in a thoroughly satisfying way. The cousins grow up 'large young women with large noses . . . the most helpless creatures at a railway-station that I ever beheld', and the eldest turns 'Tractarian and peculiar', and falls hopelessly in love with the new Rector. Even the governess is remembered, and marries the old man next door.

Six to Sixteen, as Mrs. Ewing says in the dedication, contains many of her opinions on the 'vexed question of the upbringing of girls'. It has been described as one of the best accounts of a Victorian girlhood, and though it is full of digression it is exceedingly readable. As the title suggests, it begins with its heroine at the age of six, orphaned by a cholera outbreak in India, and gives an account of her up to the age of sixteen. There are some shrewd observations in it on the pains of adolescence and the wrong-headedness of girls' schools (a lot of which still applies), and a delightful account of the education and activities of two girls at a Yorkshire rectory, which includes much autobiographical detail. Mrs. Ewing's opinion is that a good home, intellectual hobbies, and a happy family life are far better for a girl than boarding-school life.

A happy family life underlies all Mrs. Ewing's stories. She never attempted the studies of the naughty, unhappy child, shunned by the rest of its family, with which Mrs. Molesworth was so successful (*Hoodie*, *Rosy*, *The Rectory Children*), or like Charlotte Yonge's *Countess Kate*. Her children are generous and loyal, quick to defend and help each other, and in this way even 'A Very Ill-tempered Family' is of the same spirit as 'Madam Liberality', for it is in defending the rights of her younger brothers and sisters that Isobel is led to quarrel so violently with Philip. Miss Gatty disliked this story, she felt the subject was too unpleasant, but all families quarrel, and it is salutary to read of this one, and to observe for oneself, without moralizing on the part of the author, the pettiness of it all, and yet the difficulty for either side to give way. Mrs. Ewing conveys most accurately the intensity of children's hatred—a commonplace among real children, but one that authors usually ignore.

An author must tread warily with bad behaviour in children; make the child hero behave too badly, and the child reader feels that it is all a little near the knuckle, that he is being 'got at'. This has been the fate of *Countess Kate*, the excellence of which is not on the whole appreciated by children. *A Great Emergency* contains just the right amount of naughtiness, and just the right amount of independence from the grown-up world, which, for a book written in 1874, is a remarkable degree of independence. The children in this book are the forebears of the Bastables, and like E. Nesbit, Mrs. Ewing here achieves a feeling of adventure in the small happenings of childhood.

' "You are quite old enough now, Charlie",' says the elder brother, Rupert, as the book opens, ' "to learn what to do whatever happens; so every half-holiday, when I am not playing cricket, I'll teach you presence of mind near the cucumber frame, if you're punctual. I've put up a bench."'

But Charlie decides there are not enough events to deal with at home, and with his friend Johnson, the canal-carrier's son, he runs away from home to look for them. Their adventures are not on any grand scale; they stow away on a barge that belongs to Johnson's father, and are immediately recognized by the bargemaster, who takes them with him down the canal to London, and brings them home safely. Charlie is very sorry for what he has done, especially when he finds that during his absence his house has caught fire, and that his brother and sister have risked their own lives to save Baby Cecil. The new freedom that Mrs.

Ewing's children were enjoying from the crushing sense of sin that oppressed so many of the earlier Victorian child heroes may be seen by comparing this book with *Countess Kate*, where the girl who runs away is made to feel a moral outcast, unfit to associate with other children lest she contaminates them.

The story which best sums up Mrs. Ewing's feelings about family life is 'Melchior's Dream', one of her very earliest works. The boy who wishes he was an only son dreams a terrible dream in which he becomes one. He fancies he is driving in a coach with Time as the coachman, and all his brothers and sisters beside him. Crowded by the other children, he is at first thankful when they are put down by the wayside, but he soon finds himself desolate and alone, nor will Time allow him to halt and take in the brothers and sisters that he sees outside, careworn, hardened, indifferent. Then he realizes what he has brought upon himself and upon them by his want of affection.

Mrs. Ewing's imagination did not really run to fantasy, and she was better at the allegorical type of story than she was at stories of magic in everyday life. 'The Brownies', 'Timothy's Shoes', 'Amelia and the Dwarfs', 'Benjy in Beastland' are, in the convention of the times, stories of naughty children reformed by fairy methods, and even then, with the exception of 'Timothy's Shoes', it is suggested that it was a dream after all. In all these stories it is the everyday world and the domestic detail that hold the most interest—Amelia's mother who says, 'Oh dear, oh dear-r-Ramelia!' in a hopeless way every time Amelia does something particularly vexing; the great earthquake of Lisbon that naughty Sam makes with all his sister's toys—and in 'The Brownies' the descriptions of the little boy venturing out at night, and in the early morning have the best magic:

'The moon rose like gold, and went up to the heavens like silver, flooding the moors with a pale ghostly light, taking the colour out of the heather, and painting black shadows under the stone walls.'

Likewise, in 'Timothy's Shoes', the description of Timothy gathering kingcups in the marsh is what one remembers, not the magic of the shoes, for they are a very matter of fact sort of magic, that keep Timothy in the right path and prevent him from playing truant, and perhaps the most interesting moment in their history is when, having been at last outgrown, they patter out of the house and away for ever.

In the collection of stories called *Old Fashioned Fairy Tales*, there is little fantasy, but a great deal of sound common sense. Mrs. Ewing had set out to compose stories in the direct tradition of the old fairy stories. These are concise, epigrammatic, witty, and completely free from sentimentality. When the Fool sets up house with the Knave, he finishes in the village stocks, robbed of all his possessions, even his clothes. 'It was very hard on the Fool; but what can one expect if he keeps company with a Knave?' And when the farmer decides to exchange his christening gift of good luck for inexhaustible gold, true, he marries the King's daughter, but on their triumphal drive there is no Good Luck to warn him of a loose stone in the arch under which they are passing. 'He wore a casque of pure gold, but his neck was broken.' But perhaps they lack appeal for children, they are too full of good sense, more fable than story.

For my part, I feel that Mrs. Ewing's most successful attempt at fantasy—apart from 'Snap-Dragons', mentioned in an earlier chapter—occurs in a not wholly successful story—'Father Hedgehog and his Neighbours'. The delightful hedgehog family are witnesses of a human drama which it would require a full-length novel to do justice to, and one tends to skip these episodes in search of the hedgehogs. Mrs. Ewing was not fettered by a feeling for the need of scientific accuracy, as her mother had been; though every detail of the hedgehog lives was as correct as she could make it, she invented complete personalities for them all, and some delicious dialogue:

' "Will the donkey be cooked when he is fat?" asked my mother.

"I smell valerian," said my father, on which she put out her nose, and he ran at it with his prickles. He always did this when he was annoyed with any of his family; and though we knew what was coming, we are all so fond of valerian, we could never resist the temptation to sniff, just on the chance of there being some about.'

Similarly, in *A Week Spent in a Glass Pond*, in which the narrator is a Great Water Beetle, and which was probably only intended to teach children to look after their aquariums properly, Mrs. Ewing describes life from a water beetle's point of view with great perception:

'And if you want peace and quiet, where can one bury oneself so safely and completely as in the mud? A state of existence, without mud at the bottom, must be a life without repose.'

But the book that has the most magic in it, that one tends to think of as one of the fairy stories, is a book that is purely domestic—*Mrs. Overtheway's Remembrances*. With most of those who love Mrs. Ewing it is the favourite book, which distils the essence of her charm. It has both light and shadow —and if the mid-Victorian books had too much shadow then the mid-twentieth century ones have too much light; rarely has anyone blended the two so well. There is the sadness of the small Ida, pressing her face to the window, and in her loneliness inventing a friendship between herself and the old lady opposite, and the happiness of family life and affections described by Mrs. Overtheway in her reminiscences. The vividness of the details of that childhood, long past even when Ida was being told of it, is entrancing. Mrs. Ewing excelled at conveying a sense of the passing of time, which is a thing many children find it difficult to believe in. But to read the story 'Mrs. Moss', the first of the 'remembrances' that Mrs. Overtheway tells Ida, is to realize, perhaps for the first time, what old age means—that old people are not born old. Mrs. Overtheway as a child longs to meet a woman whom her elders describe as the great beauty of her grandmother's time. She imagines her radiant in white brocade and pea-green satin, with powdered hair, dancing a minuet. But when she finally meets her, Mrs. Moss is old, stooping, and ugly, with a hairy chin. To a child this is a sudden revelation.

Perhaps 'Reka Dom' is the 'remembrance' where the undiluted joy of the best moments of childhood shines through most clearly. It was written from Canada, from the house on the river that she and her husband had called 'Reka Dom' after a house that she and her sister had seen in Devon. The story is compounded of the intense happiness of those two honeymoon years in Canada, and at the same time of the deep love and nostalgia that she felt for her own home and family. The house that she describes is a child's earthly paradise, but mingled with all the joy that the children feel is a little sadness; what has become of the little Russians who once lived in the house and made their gardens there, each garden in the shape of the child's initial? Then, many years later, when the children are grown up and the river house long ago abandoned, the narrator meets the little Russian whose garden she took over, and they discover each other's identities through the deep love that they each feel for 'Reka Dom'.

No one has conveyed better than Mrs. Ewing the warmth of family affection, the happy moments of childhood, the intensity of one's feelings then, but here, where she mingled them with the *lachrimae rerum*, she touched greatness.

BIBLIOGRAPHY

Nearly all Mrs. Ewing's works were first published in magazines, chiefly *Aunt Judy's Magazine*, and were reprinted in book form by the S.P.C.K. or by George Bell & Sons. These included, besides stories, a certain number of short articles, poems, and translations, a full list of which can be found in *Juliana Horatia Ewing and her Books*, by H. K. F. Gatty, though the dates in this work are not always accurate. The list that follows includes all Mrs. Ewing's stories; the articles and translations were all reprinted in Miscellanea, vol. xvii of the S.P.C.K. collected works, and the poems and songs in *Verses for Children, and Songs for Music*, vol. ix. Vol. xviii, *J. H. Ewing, her Books and Letters* contains, as well as Miss Gatty's memoir (reprinted) a selection of Mrs. Ewing's letters.

PRINCIPAL WORKS OF MRS. EWING

(the dates given in square brackets refer to the original publication in magazines).

Melchior's Dream and Other Tales, 1862: (Melchior's Dream [1861], A Bit of Green [1861], The Blackbird's Nest [1861], Friedrich's Ballad, The Viscount's Friend); 1885 Edition (The Yew Lane Ghosts [1865], A Bad Habit [1877], a Happy Family [1883], added).

Mrs. Overtheway's Remembrances, 1869 [1866-8].

The Brownies and Other Tales, 1870: (The Brownies [1865], An Idyll of the Wood [1867], Three Christmas Trees [1867], The Land of Lost Toys [1869], Christmas Crackers [1869-70], Amelia and the Dwarfs [1870]).

A Flat Iron for a Farthing, 1872 [1870-71].

Lob Lie-by-the-fire, or The Luck of Lingborough, and Other Tales, 1874: (Lob Lie-by-the-fire, Benjy in Beastland [1870], Timothy's Shoes [1870-71], The Peace Egg [1871], Old Father Christmas [1873]).

Six to Sixteen, 1875 [1872].

Jan of the Windmill, 1876 [The Miller's Thumb, 1872-3].

A Great Emergency and Other Tales, 1877: (A Great Emergency [1874], Madam Liberality [1873], A Very Ill-tempered Family [1874-5], Our Field [1876]).

We and the World, 1880 [1877-79].

Old Fashioned Fairy Tales, 1882: (Kind William and the Water Sprite [1869], The Cobbler and the Ghosts [1870], The Nix in Mischief [1870], The Hillman and the Housewife [1870], The Neck [1870], The First Wife's Wedding Ring [1870], The Magic Jar [1870], The Widows and the Strangers [1871], The Laird and the Man of Peace [1871], The Ogre Courting [1871], Murdoch's Rath [1872], The Magician's Gifts [1872], Knave and Fool [1872], The Fiddler in the Fairy Ring [1873], Good Luck is Better than Gold [1875], I Won't [1876], The Magician Turned Mischief Maker [1876]).

Brothers of Pity and Other Tales of Beasts and Men, 1822: (Brothers of Pity [1877], Among the Merrows [1872], Toots and Boots [1876], Father Hedgehog and his Neighbours [1876], Flaps [1879]. As vol. xii in the collected works 1894-96, this book also included Tiny's Tricks and Toby's Tricks [1885] and The Owl in the Ivy Bush [1885].

Blue and Red, or The Discontented Lobster, 1883 [1881].

A Week Spent in a Glass Pond by the Great Water Beetle, 1883 [1876].

Jackanapes, 1883 [1879].

Daddy Darwin's Dovecote, 1884 [1881].

The Story of a Short Life, 1885 [Laetus Sorte Mea, or, The Story of a Short Life, 1882].

Mary's Meadow, 1886: (Mary's Meadow [1883-4], Letters from a Little Garden [1884-5]). *Mary's Meadow and Other Tales of Fields and Flowers,* vol. xvi of collected works 1894-96 also included Sunflowers and a Rushlight [1882], reprinted for the first time.

Dandelion Clocks, and Other Tales, 1887: (Dandelion Clocks [1876], The Blind Hermit and the Trinity Flower [1871], The Kyrkegrim Turned Preacher [1875], The Blind Man and the

Talking Dog [1876], Ladders to Heaven [1877], So-so [1878]).
The Peace Egg, and a Christmas Mumming Play, 1887.
Snap-Dragons, and Old Father Christmas, 1888 (Snap-Dragons, 1870].
Verses for Children, 3 vols. 1888 (first issued in 24 quarto vols., 1883-5).
Works, 18 vols., 1894-96.

BIOGRAPHY

Horatia K. F. Gatty: *Juliana Horatia Ewing and her Books*, 1885.
Mrs. Marshall: *A.L.O.E. and Mrs. Ewing*, 1897.
Christabell Maxwell: *Mrs. Gatty and Mrs. Ewing*, 1949.
Marghanita Laski: *Mrs. Ewing, Mrs. Molesworth, and Mrs. Hodgson Burnett*, 1950.

AMERICAN EDITIONS OF
BOOKS BY MRS. EWING

Brownies and Other Stories, illustrated by Ernest H. Shepard. Children's Illustrated Classic, E. P. Dutton, 1954.
Jackanapes, illustrated by Tasha Tudor. Henry Z. Walck, 1948. Everyman's Library Edition, E. P. Dutton, 1954.
Jan of the Windmill, illustrated by Mrs. Allingham. Henry Z. Walck, 1960.